SERGEANT SHAKESPEARE

SERGEANT
SHAKESPEARE

DUFF COOPER

London
RUPERT HART-DAVIS
1949

Printed in Great Britain by Richard Clay and Company, Ltd.,
Bungay, Suffolk

To Diana

I told you once that Shakespeare had been in the army, that he had served in the Low Countries and had been promoted to non-commissioned rank. You hesitated to believe me; so now that I have a little leisure, I am going to prove it.

First I must explain how the knowledge came to me. It was during the first of the two wars which, in our time, the German people have waged against the civilised world. The battalion was in the line, and on that night the company in which I was a second-lieutenant was 'in support'. I was sleeping soundly when I heard the voice of the company-commander giving the order 'Wake up that officer and tell him to put on his gas mask'. The small recess in the side of the bank where I was lying was concealed by a hanging blanket, so that my hasty search for the gas mask, which should have been firmly fixed to my chest, but which, preferring comfort to security, I had laid aside, was not detected. Having adjusted it with difficulty, I stumbled out into the night. It was dark but I could see standing in groups my hideously disguised companions. It was impossible to distinguish between them or even to tell which were officers, for in those days officers and men wore the same uniform in the line.

I gathered that gas shells were supposed to have

fallen. I doubted it. An expert is needed to tell the difference between the various vile smells that come from bursting shells. Genuine experts were rare, and the less genuine preferred, rightly, to err on the side of caution. I asked one of the silent forms beside me whether there had been any casualties. A sepulchral voice came from the gas mask and replied, 'Only Sergeant Shakespeare, who was killed instantly by the explosion of the shell'. There, on the fields of Flanders, the name seemed to strike some dim echo out of the past.

The worst of gas alarms was that those who had been responsible for sounding them were naturally reluctant to give the 'all clear' signal. A premature sniff to test the atmosphere might prove fatal, and, if all were well too soon, there might be suspicion of a false alarm. On this occasion for an hour or more we stood about, grimly gazing at one another without recognition while the stars faded and the summer night gave way to dawn.

Sergeant Shakespeare had only recently rejoined the battalion, having been wounded earlier in the war. I hardly knew him, and it was not of him that I was thinking during the long vigil. His name had started off another train of thought. I was not fond of soldiering, and I was eagerly longing for the end of the war. It occurred to me that Shakespeare had been fortunate to live in an age when world wars and military conscription were unknown. Homesick as I was, it seemed to me that nothing could be pleasanter than to pass a lifetime between London and Warwickshire. Nor could it have been dull, for those were stirring times. Shakespeare must have been a young man at the time of the Armada. He must have been there on that memorable night when the beacons flared from one end of England to the other, calling the citizens to arms. It was strange that I could remember no passage in his works that recalled what must have been one of the great emotions of his life. Nor could I think of any description of the feeling of a whole people awaiting invasion by an overwhelmingly powerful foe. Most of the fighting that I could recollect in the plays took place in foreign countries, and particularly in France. That seemed odd. However, there was much that I had never read. I must read more after the war. I had a pocket edition of the Comedies in my haversack. I could get on with that meanwhile.

The day broke, and soon we were marching up to the relief of another company in the front line. It was a perfect morning, and I was surprised to find corn growing so close to the battlefield. The crops were of course neglected and the poppies, which were rife, added to the beauty of the scene. I had that light-hearted exhilaration which comes sometimes after insufficient sleep. I decided that I would read *Love's Labour's Lost*—a play that I knew very little, and which had seemed to me when I had once read, or tried to read, it, too fanciful, too artificial, too remote from the workaday world.

7

The front line was held very lightly in the summer of 1918. A company would be spread out in a number of small posts separated from one another by a quarter or even half a mile. It was the business of an officer during his tour of duty to visit each of these posts at least once, in order to ensure that all was in order, sentries awake, and machine-guns properly placed. Between tours of duty officers had nothing to do but to sleep or feed. And even during tours of duty, I must tell you frankly, there were some officers who would pause in the deserted trench between one post and another, and, pulling a volume from the pocket, would sit down on the fire-step for a quarter-of-an-hour, and escape into the forest of Arden, a wood near Athens, or the park of the King of Navarre.

It was in these circumstances, then, that I set myself for the first time to the serious reading of *Love's Labour's Lost*. I knew that it was one of Shakespeare's earliest comedies, if not the first, and I felt confident that in its pages I should find nothing that could remind me of the life that I was leading or the occupation that I liked to forget. Nor did a military metaphor occurring in the first dozen lines of the play distress me:

LLL i 8   Therefore, brave conquerors,—for so you are,
That war against your own affections
And the huge army of the world's desires.[1]

---

[1] The text used throughout this book is that of the original Temple Shakespeare.

8

These fine verses did not recall me to the trenches, but when, a little further in the same play, I came upon the word 'corporal', I was startled. Perhaps it was because I had just been speaking to a corporal. Whatever the cause, I was vaguely annoyed that a corporal should have been dragged into Berowne's highly fantastic attack upon the God of love. After denouncing Cupid as:

> Liege of all loiterers and malcontents,
> Dread prince of plackets, king of codpieces,

LLL iv 1 182

he concludes with bathos by calling him a general, and bewails that he himself should have to serve under such an officer in the humble rank of corporal.

There is no reason to suppose that Berowne had been a soldier, nor any cause why he should slip so easily into military metaphor. 'Have at you, then, affection's men at arms'—so he apostrophises his companions; and before the meeting between these young lords, sworn to misogyny, and the Princess with her ladies, he exhorts them:

> Advance your standards, and upon them, lords;
> Pell-mell, down with them! but be first advised,
> In conflict that you get the sun of them.

LLL iv 3 368

The impression that these words made upon me when I then read them was profound, because only a few days before I had heard a musketry instructor expounding to his squad, at what seemed to me inordinate length, the very obvious undesirability of firing with the sun in their eyes. Why

9

should such language slip so easily from the tongue of a young poet who had never seen a shot fired, and who was treating of romantic love affairs between lords and ladies at a king's court?

My reading on that occasion was not finished without once more being recalled with a jerk to my actual surroundings. Don Armado, the 'fantastical Spaniard', is talking with his page, Moth, 'seated beneath the trees'. The pair are reminiscent of another even more fantastical Spaniard who had not yet come into being and who held similar conversations with his equally practical follower. Moth makes use of the expression 'As swift as lead'. The Don enquires, 'Is not lead a metal heavy, dull, and slow?' To which Moth replies, 'Is that lead slow which is fired from a gun?' A jest which did not lack point when read in the trenches.

Walter Bagehot in an essay on Shakespeare [1] quotes from *Venus and Adonis* a description of hare-hunting, and adds 'It is absurd to say we know *nothing* about the man who wrote that; we know that he had been after a hare'. And the same writer, dealing with Shakespeare's knowledge of nature, insists that 'What truly indicates excellent knowledge, is the habit of constant, sudden, and almost unconscious allusion, which implies familiarity, for it can arise from that alone'. If we can discover such allusion to military matters running through the works of Shakespeare, if it is more frequent in

---

[1] *Literary Studies*, vol. 1, p. 131.

the earlier than in the later ones, and if there is
nothing in the known facts of his life that renders
it improbable, may we not conclude that he served
in the army, or must we seek some more recondite
and less likely explanation ?

But before I go any further towards proving to you that Shakespeare was a soldier it were well to determine what claims he has upon our interest. During the nineteenth century a great many ingenious theories were conceived concerning the authorship of Shakespeare's works. Such theories, 'the cankers of a calm world and a long peace', although most of them have been exploded, have left doubts in the minds of the ignorant which had better be dispelled. If William Shakespeare were only a man who came from Warwickshire to London, and there hung about the entrances to theatres, holding horses for the gentry, until in the pursuit of this not very remunerative occupation he acquired so large a fortune that he was able to go home again and settle down as a wealthy country gentleman; then, strange as his career must have been, neither you nor I would wish to study it, or care whether he joined the army or remained a civilian.

You will have heard stories that all sorts of people were really responsible for the works of Shakespeare. The name of Francis Bacon has been mentioned and those of the Earls of Derby and Oxford and of Roger Manners, Earl of Rutland. I think you were at one time inclined to favour this last claimant, without having studied the evidence very closely. Unfortunately he was barely sixteen years old when Shakespeare had already obtained such fame and popularity as to have incurred the wrath of a rival poet, Robert Greene, who published an attack on him in 1592. Rutland did not impress his contemporaries as being a clever man —rather the reverse [1]—and he died at the age of thirty-six, so I fear that his marriage to the daughter of Sir Philip Sidney must remain his most important link with English literature.

You may be struck by the fact that all these imaginary Shakespeares should have been noblemen. The explanation is simple. The inventors of the theories must seek to show that the facts and dates in the lives of their pretenders fit in with the few facts and dates that are known in the history of the writing and production of Shakespeare's plays. But we have got few facts or dates concerning the lives of any except great noblemen at that period. Therefore the search must be restricted to that one very limited category. Some who doubt Shakespeare's authorship of his works have found it strange that we should know so little about the life of so great a man. But we do, in fact, know more about Shakespeare than about most writers of the period. It was not then considered that the private lives of humble authors were matters of interest.

I am not, however, here concerned to disprove

---

[1] He became involved in Essex's conspiracy—1601—but was considered to be of slight importance and escaped with a heavy fine. (Comtesse de Chambrun, *Shakespeare Retrouvé*, p. 276.)

the various claims to Shakespearean authorship which have been, from time to time, put forward. Clever men can prove all kinds of nonsense, and extremely ingenious evidence has been produced in favour of a number of candidates. But it has always seemed to me most necessary, before showing that somebody else wrote Shakespeare's works, to prove that he did not write them himself. This nobody has ever done.

The nineteenth century had a touching belief in the efficacy of education. The men of that period did not like to believe that the greatest of all writers was ill-educated. No manuscripts of Shakespeare's survive. From this fact learned men deduce that he could not write. It were as sensible to argue that because we have none of his boots he could not walk. There is no mention of his books in his will, therefore he cannot have had any. But how many testators do refer to their books as apart from their other goods and chattels ? A few bibliophiles, perhaps, but it is very rare for a great writer to be a bibliophile. Shakespeare, we are told, had not travelled, yet most of the plays are laid in foreign countries. In the first place we do not know that he had not travelled, and in the second place the author who lays a scene on the sea-coast of Bohemia, and who makes a character depend on the tide in order to sail by sea from Verona to Milan was not a great traveller. He wrote two plays about Venice. In neither of them is there the slightest suggestion that 'the sea's the street there' or even that the Rialto is a 'bridge with houses on it, where they kept the carnival'. It is argued that he was not learned. Neither was the man who made the clock strike in *Julius Caesar* and introduced cannon into the reign of King John. It is possible that young Lord Rutland might have committed such howlers, but not Francis Bacon, Lord Verulam, Viscount St. Albans, Lord Chancellor of England.

If those who seek to sustain this argument are to prove anything of value, they must establish not that Shakespeare was an ill-educated man, which was recognised by his contemporaries and which leads nowhere, but that he was both so ignorant and so lacking in intelligence as to render it quite impossible for him to have produced the works that are attributed to him. In all historical enquiry one ounce of contemporary testimony is worth a million tons of learned speculation. Among all the professors who have devoted their lives to the study of Shakespeare there is not one who knows so much about him as the meanest scene-shifter at the Globe Theatre knew. Fortunately we possess contemporary evidence concerning Shakespeare—not in abundance, but in sufficient quantity to correct some of the more egregious errors of the learned.

Shakespeare lived the greater part of his life in the small, brilliant literary society which illuminated London at the end of the sixteenth and the beginning of the seventeenth century. Never before nor since have so many men of genius lived together in such close propinquity. Everybody knew everybody. No man of talent could escape the close scrutiny or the shrewd comments of a score of rivals, competing, like himself, for the favour of the Queen, the Court and the public. In that galaxy of fierce competition Shakespeare rapidly soared into the highest orbit. Literary men have never been noted for their indulgence towards one another, nor for their over-enthusiastic admiration for the work of their rivals. But apart from the violent attack made upon him by Robert Greene, which has been already mentioned, Shakespeare escaped criticism. This was the more surprising in view of the success which he so rapidly acquired, and so long retained. There seems to have been some sweet and lovable quality in his nature, which disarmed envy and which enthroned this ill-educated dramatist not only in public opinion and at Court but also in the hearts of his friends.

At the Mermaid Tavern all the poets and wits of the age—and what an age!—met daily and nightly. Conversation at the Mermaid was a better test of intelligence than all the examination papers that were ever set. More was needed than 'small Latin and less Greek' if a man would hope to hold his own when the cup was flowing among those 'bards of passion and of mirth'. Can it be imagined for a moment that if Shakespeare had been the dolt that the doltish Baconians believe him to have been, the fact would have escaped the notice of those keen and jealous eyes with which less successful competitors were ever watching him ? Many good writers are poor conversationalists, and if Shakespeare had taken little part in these battles of wit, it would not prove anything, nor certainly 'write him down an ass', but his contemporaries might have noted it, and their suspicions would have been aroused. We possess, however, convincing testimony to the contrary.

Thomas Fuller was still a boy when Shakespeare died, but he was already picking up the literary gossip of the immediate past. He became preacher at the Savoy, and must have known, as a young man, any number of Shakespeare's intimate friends. He writes of Shakespeare in his *Worthies of England*, 'Many were the wit combats between him and Ben Jonson which two I behold like a Spanish great gallion and an English man-of-war. Master Jonson, like the former, was built far higher in learning; solid but slow in his performances. Shakespeare like the English man-of-war, lesser in bulk but lighter in sailing, could turn with all tides, tack about and take advantage of all winds, by the quickness of his wit and invention.' [1]

Ben Jonson was not an easy companion. He was vain of his learning, inclined to be dominating and had once killed a man in a quarrel. Of all his competitors Shakespeare was the most formidable. Two men in such circumstances might easily have been enemies. The sparring of wits might easily have inflicted wounds and left scars. Yet they were friends, and remained so. When Shakespeare

[1] Thomas Fuller, *Worthies of England*, 1662.

retired to Stratford, Jonson visited him there, and the occasion was celebrated so heartily that it may have brought on the illness from which Shakespeare died. After his death it was Ben Jonson who wrote the dedicatory ode in the first folio. Is it possible to believe that Ben Jonson devoted his time and affection to one whom he knew to be a fool and an impostor? Or are we, on the other hand, to suppose that in such intimate relations, extending over so many years, Shakespeare was able successfully to deceive Jonson? If he were clever enough to do that he must have been a very remarkable man, but, if he were a very remarkable man, there is no reason why he should not have written his works.

Jonson was not alone in contributing laudatory verse to the first edition of Shakespeare's collected works. Hugh Holland, Leonard Digges and James Mabbe, all distinguished men and accomplished poets, expressed themselves with even greater enthusiasm. Dryden, writing in the same century, found fault with Jonson's panegyric, pointing out that it was concerned rather with Shakespeare's character than with his work. If there be force in this criticism it goes to show that Jonson, while won by the charm of the man, either retained some streaks of jealousy, or else genuinely lacked enthusiasm for the writer. It is easy for contemporaries to form faulty estimates of one another's work, but it is impossible for contemporaries to mistake an illiterate peasant for a writer of the first rank.

We have not finished with the fantasies of Shakespearean scholarship when we have demolished the case of those who believe that Shakespeare was incapable of writing his own works. For drawn up in battle against those who hold that Shakespeare was too stupid to have written anything at all is a more formidable company, who maintain that Shakespeare was such an exceptional genius that he was incapable of writing anything that was not of the very highest quality, and that therefore any passages in his plays that seem unworthy of him must be the work of other hands. It is with greater trepidation that I approach a subject which has occupied so much of the time and labour of so many devoted Shakespearean experts. It is necessary, however, for me to do so, for much of the material on which my case is based must be drawn from plays or passages whose Shakespearean authorship is questioned.

Surely here again, as in the case of the Baconians and their kindred tribes, the original assumption, upon which the whole vast fabric of erudition is based, is open to question. Because Shakespeare was the greatest of poets are we justified in asserting that he was incapable of occasionally writing what King George III not inaccurately described as 'poor stuff'? Two thousand years ago Horace recorded, with regret, that even Homer sometimes nodded. Why should what was true of Homer be false of Shakespeare? We know nothing of the conditions in which Homer worked, but we know that Shakespeare was writing for the theatre, that his output was large and that his time was short. Often he must have been working in haste on a play that had to be ready for a certain date. Often he must have had to think of his actors, and always of his public. Padding was sometimes necessary. He could not always choose his themes. Tragedy may have been demanded when he was feeling gayest, and light comedy when his heart was being torn into shreds. Every circumstance was present that would tend to produce unequal writing. Compare his lot with that of two other of our great poets, Wordsworth and Tennyson. They were their own masters. Neither poverty nor public jogged their elbows. They had ample time for revision. Yet both of them, true poets though they were, produced, on occasion, stuff that was worse than poor: uninspired pedestrian drivel, seeming to be the product of a writer totally bereft of poetic feeling.

The facts, for which we have to find an explanation, are that in many of Shakespeare's plays occur passages which are not so good as the rest, and that some of the plays are very inferior to others. There are three hypotheses which suggest themselves. The first is that Shakespeare was a very unequal writer, that he was often writing under great pressure, and that he sometimes wrote very badly indeed. There is surely nothing very unlikely in this ?

The second hypothesis is that this man of stupendous genius would sometimes feel the need of a helping hand. He would then apply to one or another of the leading writers of the day, his own keen rivals, who would obligingly come along and hammer out some verses, always extremely bad ones, which the great poet, who could do so much better himself, would gratefully accept and duly embody in his play. I find this theory impossible to swallow. A writer is always more likely to be tolerant of his own bad work than of the bad work of others, and more inclined to shirk the effort of improving a passage he has written himself than to mar his work by the deliberate insertion of poor material supplied by another.

The third explanation is that Shakespeare would get hold of a play written by somebody else and would rewrite it. In doing so he would occasionally leave whole passages of the original unaltered, these of course being the passages which critics are unwilling to believe that he wrote. Now we know that on one occasion something of this sort actually happened. The play in question was called *The Troublesome Raigne of John, King of England*. It was not a bad play, and it was anonymous. Shakespeare re-wrote it under the title of *King John*. He followed the old play closely in its treatment of historical fact but he left not a line unchanged. It is interesting to compare the two and to note with what seeming ease he converts dross into gold. For instance, the famous closing lines:

> Come the three corners of the world in arms,
> And we shall shock them. Nought shall make us rue,
> If England to itself do rest but true.

These are plainly based on the following couplet which occurs in the earlier play:

> If England's peers and people join in one,
> Nor Pope, nor France, nor Spain can do them wrong.

Because Shakespeare followed this method upon one occasion there is no reason to suppose, without evidence in support of this supposition, that he followed it upon others. Nor upon this occasion did he treat his material as some would have us believe that he treated it upon others, leaving great wads of it unaltered and unimproved. Nor was this the work of one of his distinguished contemporaries, who are supposed tamely to have submitted to their plays being re-written by Shakespeare.

It is particularly upon the earliest and upon some of the latest plays that scholars have pounced as affording proof that lesser men than Shakespeare were engaged upon the task of producing his works. To simple beings, unencumbered by excessive learning, it would not seem surprising that a young man's earliest artistic efforts should be inferior to those of his maturity, nor impossible that, as the end of the journey approaches, the style should undergo a change, and that signs of fatigue should become apparent.

Henry VI, Part I, is the first of Shakespeare's historical plays, and it is in many ways the least admirable. I shall return to it later and deal with it at greater length, because it supports other parts of my contention. Here let it merely be said—and it can hardly be questioned—that the play bears the mark of apprenticeship. It is crude, but it is full of gusto. There is good poetry in it, but little stagecraft. It is exactly what might be expected of a young writer with great talent, but with no experience. But so simple and reasonable an explanation is not good enough for those who delight in finding elaborate solutions for the problems they set themselves. So the play has been passed through the strange alembic of all the scientific tests that the ingenuity of modern scholarship has devised, with the result that we are asked to believe that this obviously immature work is the product of the combined intelligence of Christopher Marlowe, Thomas Kyd, Robert Greene, George Peele, Thomas Nashe, Thomas Lodge, and Shakespeare himself.[1] All these men were accomplished writers and poets, some of them were exquisite poets, and to believe that they all got together, in some inexplicable manner, to collaborate on a

---

[1] Professor Dowden's preface to *Henry VI, Part I* in *The Histories and Poems of Shakespeare* (Oxford, 1915), pp. 453–4, where all the theories held by different scholars concerning the authorship of the play are reviewed.

play, which turned out to be a poor one, and that they then fathered it on Shakespeare, the beginner, surely demands a greater degree of credulity than to believe that in this first attempt Shakespeare showed the faults of inexperience, which we can see him overcoming in the very superior second and third parts of the same history?

That is an example taken from the beginning of Shakespeare's literary career. Here is another taken from the end of it. *Henry VIII* is a very different play from *Henry VI, Part I*. It was one of the last of the plays, and the style of the verse differs in some respects from that of the others. The ordinary person will not be astonished that an author in the course of writing thirty-seven plays should alter his style, but such a phenomenon arouses the gravest suspicions in the mind of a scholar. It seems that Tennyson, in an idle moment, let fall the remark that there was much in this play that reminded him of the poetry of Fletcher. Unfortunately he was overheard by a learned commentator, James Spedding, an authority on Bacon, but not a Baconian. Like a bloodhound given a trail, he instantly fell upon it, and never relinquished the quest until he had produced a book which sets out to prove that practically the whole play, and many of the most famous passages in it, were the work of Fletcher, and that Shakespeare's contribution was quite inconsiderable. That was a hundred years ago, and ever since this view has been widely accepted. The case is based solely upon what are called metrical tests. I will not weary you by explaining in detail what these tests are. Suffice it to say that they are concerned with such matters as the occurrence of a redundant syllable at the end of a line, and the place where a break occurs in the middle of it. If it can be shown to a scholar that certain mannerisms of this sort occur far more frequently in the works of Fletcher than in those of Shakespeare, and that in this play they are more frequent than in any of Shakespeare's other plays, then the scholar is satisfied that the play which was universally attributed to Shakespeare, and was acted and published under his name, was really the work of Fletcher.

There are, of course, other explanations. Many great poets have deliberately varied their technique in later life. Shakespeare may have done so. Or he may have been recently reading some of Fletcher's plays, and have unwittingly caught the lilt of his music. Either of these commends itself to me rather than the mathematical tests applied by the experts.

But there is one argument against the theory of Fletcher's authorship which to my mind is conclusive. Fletcher, a respectable man, the son of a bishop, wrote a large number of plays, some in partnership with Beaumont, some independently. He never sought to conceal his collaboration with Beaumont. Why should he seek to conceal his collaboration with Shakespeare, then at the height of his fame and success? Why should he connive at a fraud? Fletcher was a good poet and a good dramatist, but if he were the author of *Henry VIII*, it was the best play he ever wrote. Is it in the nature of man, is it above all in the nature of literary men, to allow a man's best work to pass without protest under the name of another? Fletcher was alive when the play was produced in 1613. He was alive ten years later when it was first published in the collected edition of Shakespeare's works. On neither the former occasion nor the latter did he lay claim to its authorship. In the portion of this play attributed to Fletcher come the grand lines:

Cromwell, I charge thee, fling away ambition:
By that sin fell the angels; how can man then,
The image of his Maker, hope to win by it?

If Fletcher wrote that and permitted it to pass as Shakespeare's he had certainly flung away ambition to some tune.

Seven years after Shakespeare's death Heminge and Condell, who had no doubt been diligently engaged on the task during the interval, published a collected edition of his works, the famous First Folio. These two men were his closest friends, they were actors who had been associated with him throughout his professional career, and they were both remembered in his will. Great pains had been taken with this book, which was a very fine production for the period, and we may be sure that the two editors, living in the very heart of the theatrical world, would not willingly have included anything spurious, or omitted anything genuine. Nor would

26

they have been permitted to do so. Shakespeare was fifty-two when he died; therefore the majority of his contemporaries were living when his works were published seven years later. Ben Jonson, Fletcher, Ford, Massinger, Chapman, Marston, Lodge, Drayton, were all vigorous. And so was Bacon. If this stout volume contained nothing that Shakespeare had written it was the most gigantic swindle ever perpetrated, and it is inconceivable that all the brilliantly clever men of that small world were either unaware of it, or carried the secret with them to the grave. It is only a little less improbable that any substantial portion of the plays should have been the work of other hands, especially of men still living.

Shakespeare had never been concerned, as Jonson was, carefully to revise his writings. It is certain that there are many corrupt passages, and it is likely that here and there lines may have crept in to the text which have no place there. Actors are apt to take liberties with their script, as Shakespeare knew, for he begged them not to.[1] Unauthorized lines were doubtless often scribbled into the prompter's copy, which afterwards became the only one available. It would be foolish to become a fundamentalist and to treat every line of the folio as holy writ, which does not admit of amendment. But of one thing we may be certain. Heminge and Condell knew better what Shakespeare wrote and what he didn't write than anybody alive

---

[1] Hamlet, 3. 2. 42.

today, or who has lived since they died. What they attributed to him was received with general agreement by his contemporaries, and I, for one, am prepared to 'take their word for a thousand pound'.

And tell me now, sweet friend, what happy gale
Blows you to Padua here from old Verona?

asks Hortensio of Petruchio in the first act of *The Taming of the Shrew*. The latter answers:

Such wind as scatters young men through the world,
To seek their fortunes farther than at home,
Where small experience grows.

It was such a breeze that on a certain day in the year 1584 or 1585 blew young William Shakespeare out of Stratford-on-Avon. He had good reason to seek his fortune elsewhere, for his start in life had not been altogether propitious. His father, a prosperous citizen, who had played a leading part in municipal life, and had at one time applied for a coat-of-arms, had come down in the world during his son's childhood. William himself had married at the age of eighteen a young woman several years older than himself, who had borne him a daughter a few months after the ceremony. Eighteen months later she had borne him twins, and it does not appear that the young man, practising no trade and qualified for no profession, can have had the means of supporting a wife and a growing family. Also there had been a scandal connected with deer-poaching. The full details will never now be known, but it seems probable that

Shakespeare was mixed up in it, and he may well have rendered himself liable to prosecution.

The twins were baptized on February 2nd, 1585, so we may be certain that Shakespeare was at home during the previous summer, and we may hope that he put off his departure until the christening of his children, possibly until his own twenty-first birthday in April of the same year. With the record of this ceremony the curtain falls upon the first act of Shakespeare's life. When it rises again seven years later, in 1592, we find the young man, who had set out to make his fortune, already established in London as a playwright of some repute. What happened in the interval has always remained a matter of conjecture. Many and various have such conjectures been, ranging from a quiet life as a country schoolmaster to a voyage round the world with Francis Drake in the *Golden Hind*.[1]

Because Shakespeare disappeared from Stratford and reappeared in London it has been rashly assumed that he went straight from the one to the other, where he remained. It is certainly arguable that the capital of his country is the likeliest place to attract a young man in search of his fortune. But

---

[1] William Burton, an actor, whose memory might have gone back to Shakespeare's lifetime, told John Aubrey (1626–1697) the schoolmaster story (E. K. Chambers, *William Shakespeare*, vol. 1, p. 22). For the voyage of discovery we are indebted to the imagination of Mr. William Bliss (*The Real Shakespeare*, chapters 4 & 5). He is obliged to make Shakespeare run away from home at the age of thirteen in order not to miss the *Golden Hind*, but he sends him on a second voyage, to the Mediterranean, during the period with which we are here dealing.

in this case there were two special circumstances which may well have turned the wanderer's footsteps in another direction. In the first place, Shakespeare was in some trouble with the authorities. In the second place, England was at war, and the press-gang was out. In time of private trouble a young man's thoughts turn naturally to the army; in time of foreign war a patriot's duty impels him in the same direction. Shakespeare was a young man in trouble and he was a patriot. Cervantes in similar circumstances, some years before, had joined the army; Ben Jonson was to do the same thing a few years later. As the latter's biographers write —'to take arms was, for a young fellow of this type in the London of Elizabeth, an obvious resource'.[1]

In the famous soliloquy where the melancholy Jaques compared the world to a stage and the life of man to a series of parts played by an actor, there figures prominently the rôle of a soldier, as though that were the normal profession for a man to adopt when he had done with creeping unwillingly to school and inditing sonnets to his mistress' eyebrow. And why should we doubt that the young man who had left his native town, his wife and his three children should set forth,

> Seeking the bubble reputation
> Even in the cannon's mouth?

In all the forty-five years of Elizabeth's reign

---

[1] Herford and Simpson, *Ben Jonson*, vol. i, p. 7.

there was no time at which the demand for soldiers was so keen as in the year 1585. Three years before the Armada, the Queen reluctantly consented to send out what was then considered a large force to the Low Countries, and she appointed as her Commander-in-Chief, Robert, Earl of Leicester, whose principal seat was at Kenilworth, thirteen miles from Stratford-on-Avon.

Is it not much more than probable that a young man, with an able body, a stout heart and a thirst for adventure, instead of setting forth on the ninety miles walk to London, incurring the grave risk of meeting the press-gang on the road, should have preferred to walk the thirteen miles to Kenilworth, and offer himself as a voluntary recruit to one of the most remarkable men of the age?

In the middle of the eighteenth century there was still current a tradition that it was Leicester who saved Shakespeare from the wrath of those who were after him on account of the poaching incident.[1] Leicester was probably the only man in the country who could give protection against the law of the land. If such protection were given it can only have been in that year 1585. Shakespeare had not required it before. In that year Leicester himself went to the Low Countries, and three years later he was dead. But when he was desperately seeking for soldiers he could hardly be expected to help a young man of twenty-one, who had left his

---

[1] Chambers, vol. ii, p. 302.

wife and family, except on condition of his joining the forces.

The most famous of those who were to fall in the campaign was Leicester's own nephew, his sister's son, Sir Philip Sidney, who at an early age had already acquired fame as a poet and as a figure of romance. There exists a letter which Sidney wrote to a friend in the following March (1586), six months before his death. The following passage occurs in this letter, 'I wrote to you a letter by Will, my Lord of Leicester's jesting player, enclosed in a letter to my wife, and I never had answer thereof. . . . I since find that the knave delivered the letters to my lady of Leicester, but whether she sent them you or no I know not, but earnestly desire to do.' [1]

So there was a jesting player called Will in the service of the Earl of Leicester a year after Will Shakespeare left Stratford, in the vicinity of Kenilworth, at a time when Leicester was collecting recruits.

Kemp ?

Leicester was a remarkable man, whose career must remain for posterity something of a mystery, in which high politics, love affairs and crime all play their part. He could win hearts and hold them, and I think he was the man whom Elizabeth, although he deceived her, loved best and longest. In an age when deep divisions were set between classes he was famous, or notorious, for the famil-

---

[1] Harleian MSS, vol. cclxxxvii, f. 1. Quoted by William J. Thoms, F.S.A., in his essay, "Was Shakespeare ever a Soldier?" (*Three Notelets on Shakespeare*, 1865).

iarity with which he treated people of every rank. Professional jesters were everywhere welcome, and what more likely than that the youthful Shakespeare, in all the glorious springtime of his genius, should have caught the notice of the middle-aged nobleman, who had always lived well and dangerously, and had never allowed even his vaulting ambition to interfere with any of the pleasures of life?

In the following year Leicester needed a messenger, to carry not official despatches to the government but private letters to relations and friends. Leicester's whole life had been spent in a maze of political and amorous intrigue. To be his postman required tact and discretion. He would not wish to give the job to a clumsy soldier, nor to deprive himself of the services of an experienced officer. Who could be better than the jesting player, who seemed to have more brains in his head than the whole of his staff put together? He could be trusted to do nothing foolish, and his presence with the army was not essential to winning the war. Shakespeare, no doubt, volunteered for the duty, and was as glad as many soldiers have been since to break by a short visit to London the monotony of a campaign in the Low Countries.

If indeed he went on this mission it is possible that he did not return from it. It is possible that, having scented the battlefield, he found, as soldiers often have done, the air of the metropolis more congenial. Or Leicester himself may have decided that the talents of his young friend were better suited to the theatre of fancy than to the stage of life. For Leicester was one of the leading patrons of the theatre, and one of the six companies of licensed players which then existed in London was his. It is to this company that we find Shakespeare belonging when we next have authentic information about him. On Leicester's death this theatrical company passed to Lord Derby, and from him to Lord Hunsdon and the latter's son. It became the King's Company after the accession of James I. Sir Sidney Lee writes that 'it is fair to assume that this was the company which Shakespeare originally joined and adhered to through life'.[1]

Am I asking you to believe anything improbable? Let us marshal the facts and set against them the assumption. We last hear of Shakespeare in Stratford at about the time when a military force was being recruited for foreign service. We know that the commander-in-chief of that force was Lord Leicester, whose principal dwelling was thirteen miles from Shakespeare's home. We know that over a hundred years after Shakespeare's death a tradition persisted that Leicester helped him when he was in trouble. We know that Shakespeare joined the theatrical company that was originally Leicester's. I am asking you to accept that tradition and to admit the probability that rather than launch into the theatrical world of London an able-bodied

---

[1] Sir Sidney Lee, *A Life of William Shakespeare*, third edition, p. 36.

young man—possibly wanted by the law—Leicester, in need of soldiers, thought it better to employ him first in the army. It is admittedly an assumption. But it is not a wild one. If it were true we should expect to find in Shakespeare's early works some evidence of his military training.

If a young man, with great talent but with little knowledge of life, recently returned from a campaign abroad, were to set himself down to write a play, it is probable that that play would strongly resemble *King Henry VI, Part I*. A fight either takes place or is described in nearly every scene of it, and the whole play reeks of the camp.

Of all the reigns in English history, that of Henry VI seems to offer the least suitable subject for a play. It is one of the longest and quite the most inglorious—a squalid record of defeat abroad and civil war at home. If Shakespeare had dealt with it last in his historical sequence, he could at least have continued the theme which runs through *Richard II*, *Henry IV* and *Henry V*, showing how there was a curse upon the House of Lancaster on account of the crime of Bolingbroke 'in compassing the crown' and 'putting down Richard, that sweet lovely rose'. But whatever the reason may have been, he chose to begin with *Henry VI*, and, considering his own inexperience and the ungrateful nature of his material, he did, as Mr. Brontë might have said, 'better than likely'.[1]

---

[1] When all London was ringing with the fame of *Jane Eyre*, Charlotte Brontë informed her father she had written it and gave him some of the enthusiastic reviews to read. When he came in to tea that evening he said, 'Girls, do you know that

Whatever the merits or demerits of the play may be, the reader receives very strongly the impression that the writer of it has been in the army. Even in the first scene, which takes place at the funeral of Henry V in Westminster Abbey, the proceedings are interrupted by the arrival of a messenger from the front who gives a stirring account of the recent defeat of Lord Talbot:

> The tenth of August last this dreadful lord,
> Retiring from the siege of Orleans,
> Having full scarce six thousand in his troop,
> By three and twenty thousand of the French
> Was round encompassed and set upon.
> No leisure had he to enrank his men;
> He wanted pikes to set before his archers;
> Instead whereof sharp stakes pluck'd out of hedges
> They pitched in the ground confusedly,
> To keep the horsemen off from breaking in.

This and what follows describing Talbot's heroic fight against odds, which continues until he is stabbed in the back, is not great poetry, but it is good, vivid writing, which makes plain what has happened. In the next scene we are transported from Westminster Abbey to the French camp before Orleans. The English are besieging the city, and a French force, under the Dauphin, is endeavouring to relieve it. The French attack, and are repulsed by the English. Joan la Pucelle joins the French troops and convinces the Dauphin of

Charlotte has been writing a book, and it is much better than likely ?' Mrs. Gaskell, *Life of Charlotte Brontë*, Thornton Edition, p. 306.

her divine mission by overthrowing him in single combat.

Scene 3 brings us back to London, where in front of the Tower a violent fight takes place between the followers of the Duke of Gloucester and those of the Cardinal of Winchester. The Mayor of London appears and persuades them to stop fighting, but the two great men go off cursing and threatening one another, leaving the Mayor to conclude the scene with the enjoyable couplet:

Good God, these nobles should such stomach bear!
I myself fight not once in forty year.

Scene 4 opens on the wall of Orleans with a Master Gunner giving instructions to his Boy. The French are still holding the city, but the English are already in the suburbs. Both the city wall of the besieged and the turrets in the suburbs whence the siege is being conducted are represented on the stage. This would present a problem to the most elaborate of modern producers, but nothing daunted the youthful Shakespeare. The Master Gunner points out the turrets and tells the Boy that the English are in possession of them, to which he replies:

Father, I know; and oft have shot at them,
Howe'er unfortunate I miss'd my aim.

The Master Gunner leaves the Boy in charge with strict instructions to inform him if he sees the enemy on the turrets. The moment his back is turned the Boy announces his intention of doing nothing of the kind. He is obviously fond of shooting, and although he has been unlucky hitherto he means to try again. Then the English appear on the turrets, including Talbot, who has recovered from his wound, and has been exchanged for a French prisoner. While they are calmly discussing at what part of the city they shall launch their next attack, the Boy, who has been momentarily absent, reappears with a linstock. He can see the English, who cannot apparently see him. The audience of course can see both, and, if inclined to be unruly, would probably be shouting warnings to their fellow countrymen. The Boy discharges the ordnance and kills Lord Salisbury and Sir Thomas Gargrave. Two birds with one shot! His luck has certainly changed.

The next two scenes continue the battle. They begin with an indecisive single combat between Talbot and La Pucelle, which is followed by a series of skirmishes. They end in the complete victory of the French and the raising of the siege. So finishes the first act, and even an Elizabethan audience must have felt that, so far, they had had their money's worth.

Act II opens with a successful night attack by the English, who recapture the town. A stage direction indicates the nature of the fun. 'The French leap over the walls in their shirts. Enter, several ways, the Bastard of Orleans, Alençon and Reignier, half ready and half unready.' While they are reproaching one another for not keeping a

40

better look-out, 'enter an English soldier, crying "A Talbot, a Talbot"—They fly, leaving their clothes behind.'

There follows an amusing incident in two scenes in which the Countess of Auvergne entices Talbot into her castle with a view to kidnapping him. He pretends to be her dupe, having taken the necessary precautions. The tables are turned; she becomes his prisoner, and when she implores his pardon he readily grants it, saying:

> Nor other satisfaction do I crave,
> But only, with your patience, that we may
> Taste of your wine and see what cates you have;
> For soldiers' stomachs always serve them well.

The most dramatic historical episode in the reign of Henry VI was the plucking of the red and white roses in the Temple Garden by the partisans of the Houses of Lancaster and York. The playwright cannot miss it, so without any warning we are transferred from the fields of France to the Temple Garden, where the dispute is at its height. Shakespeare, however, does not seem interested, as Bacon would certainly have been, in the intricate legal and genealogical points at issue. When both sides ask Warwick to arbitrate between them we seem to hear the authentic voice of the young countryman, turned soldier, speaking:

> Between two hawks, which flies the higher pitch;
> Between two dogs, which hath the deeper mouth;
> Between two blades, which bears the better temper;
> Between two horses, which doth bear him best;

41

Between two girls, which hath the merriest eye;
I have perhaps some shallow spirit of judgement:
But in these nice sharp quillets of the law,
Good faith, I am no wiser than a daw.

This is a voice of which you will hear echoes throughout the plays. You will hear it in the speeches of the Bastard Faulconbridge and of Enobarbus. You will hear it at its noblest in the mouth of Hotspur, and you will detect a hideous imitation of it in that of Iago.

Having arrived in London, we remain there for two more scenes. We witness the death of the aged Mortimer in the Tower, urging with his last breath his nephew, the future Duke of York, to civil war:

Here dies the dusky torch of Mortimer,
Choked with ambition of the meaner sort.

And to the Parliament House, where you will not be surprised to hear that there is more fighting, although the King in person is presiding over the sitting. Again the Mayor makes his appearance and complains that the servants of the two factions are pelting one another with stones, so fast:

That many have their giddy brains knock'd out.

Enter serving men 'with bloody pates' who continue to fight until their leaders, the Duke and the Cardinal, are persuaded by the young king to make peace with one another, a peace which, they inform the audience in asides, neither intends to keep.

Returning to France, we find ourselves once more concerned with a siege. It is Rouen this time instead of Orleans. La Pucelle and four soldiers succeed in entering the city disguised as peasants and handing it over to the French. This perfectly legitimate *ruse de guerre* is described by the English as 'treason', 'treachery' and 'hellish mischief'. And after further fighting they drive out the French. The next scene shows the French army on the plains near Rouen—'Drum sounds afar off— Here sound an English march—Enter, and pass over at a distance, Talbot and his forces.' Two lines later—'French march. Enter the Duke of Burgundy and forces.' We cannot wonder that stage managers hesitate to reproduce *Henry VI, Part I*. La Pucelle persuades Burgundy, without much difficulty, to transfer his friendship from England to France.

In the next scene, where King Henry VI is installed in Paris, he is made to say, 'When I was young . . . I do remember how my father said. . . .' Now, if seven of the cleverest men in England had combined their intellectual resources in the writing of this play, as some believe, surely we may suppose that it would have occurred to one of them that Henry was eight months old when his father died, and therefore could not possibly have remembered hearing him say anything?

In this scene also there is a fight between a supporter of the Red Rose, at present represented by Somerset, and the White Rose already standing for York. This leads up to the death of Talbot, who is now besieging Bordeaux, and the moral of the six scenes in which, with a wealth of bloodshed, his end is described, is that he falls a victim not to the soldiers of France but to internal squabbles and jealousies amongst those who held power in England. Either Somerset or York could have saved him, but distrust of one another held back both:

> The fraud of England, not the force of France,
> Hath now entrapp'd the noble-minded Talbot.

How often in subsequent wars have British soldiers attributed their plight to the quarrels of highly placed politicians!

The arrival on the battlefield of Talbot's young son, John, and his refusal to fly, as his father implores him to do, are described with beauty and pathos.

The last act is the worst. We are shocked that Shakespeare should have described Joan of Arc [1] as a witch rather than a saint, but we cannot blame him. He was dealing with events of the previous century, and international slander dies slow. He was merely recording what he had been told. There are educated Frenchmen living who still believe that St. Helena is a plague-stricken island and that the perfidious English sent Napoleon there on account of the climate, which killed him. In point of fact the island is exceptionally salubrious, and the poor man died of cancer.

---

[1] Swinburne, who loved Joan of Arc and hated George Peele, because he had been rude about Eleanor of Castile, says that Peele must have written these scenes. (*A Study of Shakespeare*, Golden Pine Edition, p. 33.) There is no other reason to think so.

44

In the closing scenes of the play the Earl of Suffolk emerges as a character of the first importance. He falls in love with Margaret of Anjou on the battlefield, and we leave him setting forth to bring her to England as a bride for the King:

> Margaret shall now be queen, and rule the king;
> But I will rule both her, the king, and realm.

are the last words, to which the obvious rubric might be added, 'to be continued in our next'.

Now can you believe that this rollicking melodrama was put together by half-a-dozen of the most distinguished, intelligent and experienced writers of that great age? Is it not much more obviously one of the earliest efforts of an ignorant young man applying his genius to the stern limitations imposed by stagecraft? And of whatever this young man may be ignorant, he knows something of soldiers, and has overheard their talk. When, in the very first scene, the messenger is asked by one of the great lords at Westminster to explain what treachery is responsible for the losses recently incurred in France, he answers:

> No treachery; but want of men and money.
> Amongst the soldiers this is muttered,
> That here you maintain several factions,
> And whilst a field should be despatch'd and fought,
> You are disputing of your generals:
> One would have lingering wars with little cost;
> Another would fly swift, but wanteth wings;
> A third thinks, without expense at all,
> By guileful fair words peace may be obtain'd.

In every war the soldiers at the front have made the same complaints, and, alas, too often there has been good ground for them. The soldiers have changed as little in the centuries as have the politicians. Talbot when he contemptuously speaks of 'pucelle or puzzle, dauphin or dogfish' is the true ancestor of the soldiers who called Ypres 'Wipers' and Ploegstraat 'Plugstreet'. And listen to the sentry's soliloquy; 'Sirs', says the Sergeant,

> Take your places and be vigilant:
> If any noise or soldier you perceive
> Near to the walls, by some apparent sign
> Let us have knowledge at the court of guard.
> *First Sentinel.* Sergeant, you shall. (*Exit Sergeant.*)
>   Thus are poor servitors,
> When others sleep upon their quiet beds
> Constrain'd to watch in darkness, rain and cold.

Well is he named first sentinel, for his words have found an echo in the heart of every soldier who has ever done sentry-duty, since the first angel was posted outside the Garden of Eden.

I have felt forced to discuss this play at length, because it is so seldom read and never acted. Taste has changed. We know by contemporary evidence[1] that it had a very great success when it was first produced. It was what the public wanted, and its

---

[1] Nashe wrote in his *Pierce Penilesse* (1592), 'How much would it have joyed brave Talbot to think that after he had lain two hundred years in his tomb, he should triumph again on the stage, and have his bones new embalmed with the tears of ten thousand spectators (at several times) who in the tragedy that represents his person imagine they behold him fresh bleeding.'

success renders all the more absurd the supposition that a number of older dramatists, with reputations already established, would have allowed the young and unknown Shakespeare to take all the credit, if they had collaborated with him in the worst parts. That Shakespeare was a swindler, taking money and credit for a play he hadn't written, and that rival poets aided and abetted him, by concealing, to their own disadvantage, the help they had given him, is a theory which, while it has been generally accepted by Shakespearean scholars, seems to me the wildest nonsense that ever was set down in print.

I see you are beginning to yawn. You have had enough of *King Henry VI, Part I*, and you are afraid I am going to analyse the other thirty-six plays at the same length. I promise not to. I propose to show you how throughout the whole of his work Shakespeare is continually reverting to the military theme, as some men revert to their days at school or university, wherever they were happiest—or imagine, in retrospect, that they were. The military metaphor is continually cropping up, soldiers are coming on to the stage more often than they are wanted, unnecessary battles are fought, and, although many of its representatives are scoundrels, there is ever present a deep respect for the profession of arms.

The fact that this absorption in military affairs is more apparent in the early than in the later plays is significant. Professor Dover Wilson, most sympathetic and perspicacious of modern Shakespearean scholars, has remarked it. 'Among his creatures of the upper class', he writes, 'it was . . . the comic characters which first seemed fully flesh and blood, the most successful for some reason in the early plays being forceful, bluff, yet vivacious and humorous soldier-men. Perhaps Shakespeare knew someone of this type and had an admiration for him.' [1]

---

[1] J. Dover Wilson, *The Essential Shakespeare*, pp. 78–79.

Perhaps—but a far simpler explanation would be that he had served in the army himself. Writing from personal experience, I should say it was rare for young intellectuals who have been frequenting literary and theatrical circles in London to develop any enthusiasm for the fighting services. The qualities that go to the making of a good soldier do not usually arouse admiration in civilian society. To be appreciated they must be seen in the exercise of the profession, and to be treasured they must be encountered on active service. It is no doubt of Mercutio and Benedick and Petruchio that Professor Dover Wilson is thinking. Nor can there be any doubt, although it is nowhere stated, that Sir Toby Belch had held a military commission. 'O, for a stone-bow, to hit him in the eye,' he exclaims when overhearing Malvolio. He swears by 'bolts and shackles' and he is always ready to draw. While we love each of these characters for his gaiety, wit and fancy, we admire them the more for feeling that they are men of courage and character who could be relied upon in time of danger.

Why, we wonder, should Benedick have been given this military background? We are told, or rather Beatrice is told, before we see him, that 'he hath done good service in these wars'. She is not impressed, as women seldom are by military prowess. Later in the play Benedick speaks with contempt of Claudio for falling in love, although he is, of course, slipping himself in the same direction.

'I have known', he says, 'when there was no music with him but the drum and the fife; and now had he rather hear the tabor and the pipe: I have known when he would have walked ten mile a-foot to see a good armour; and now will he lie ten nights awake, carving the fashion of a new doublet. He was wont to speak plain and to the purpose, like an honest man and a soldier; and now is he turned orthography.'

There is a certain similarity about Shakespeare's soldiers. They are not the strong, silent type. Antony says to Enobarbus, 'Thou art a soldier only: speak no more', but he never persuades Enobarbus to stop talking. Hotspur talks to the end and death overtakes him before he has finished his sentence. Othello wins Desdemona's heart with the battle stories he tells her. Macbeth talks himself into cowardice, until Lady Macbeth's taunt, 'Fie, my lord, fie! A soldier, and afeard', whets his almost blunted purpose.[1]

They all have a soldierly contempt for civilians, and are inclined to undervalue the blessings of peace. 'This peace is nothing, but to rust iron, increase tailors, and breed ballad-makers', says one of the servingmen in *Coriolanus*. His companion agrees, 'Let me have war, say I; it exceeds peace as far as day does night; it's spritely, waking, audible, and full of vent . . . peace is a great maker

---

[1] This passage occurs in the sleep-walking scene, where the dreamer is plainly repeating words actually used on the night of the murder.

of cuckolds.' 'Ay,' one rejoins, 'and it makes men hate one another.' 'Reason,' says another, 'because they then less need one another. The wars for my money.'

Falstaff, contemptuously describing the men he has pressed, calls them 'such as indeed were never soldiers, but discarded unjust serving-men, younger sons to younger brothers, revolted tapsters, and ostlers trade-fallen; the cankers of a calm world and a long peace, ten times more dishonourable ragged than an old faced ancient'.

Even poor Imogen, disguised as a boy and lost in Wales, says, perhaps to keep her own courage up, 'Plenty and peace breeds cowards; hardness ever of hardiness is mother'.

But the noblest compliment ever paid to war comes, as it should, from the mouth of Othello:

Farewell the plumed troop and the big wars
That make ambition virtue! O, farewell,
Farewell the neighing steed and the shrill trump,
The spirit-stirring drum, the ear-piercing fife,
The royal banner and all quality,
Pride, pomp and circumstance of glorious war!
And, O you mortal engines, whose rude throats
The immortal Jove's dread clamours counterfeit,
Farewell! Othello's occupation's gone!

The soldier's exasperation with meddling civilians was never better expressed than by that most impatient of officers, Harry Hotspur. The King is reproaching him with having refused to hand over to him certain prisoners whom he had demanded after the battle of Holmedon.

My liege, [he protests] I did deny no prisoners.
But I remember, when the fight was done,
When I was dry with rage and extreme toil,
Breathless and faint, leaning upon my sword,
Came there a certain lord, neat, and trimly dress'd,
Fresh as a bridegroom; and his chin new reap'd
Show'd like a stubble-land at harvest-home;
He was perfumed like a milliner;
And 'twixt his finger and his thumb he held
A pouncet-box, which ever and anon
He gave his nose and took't away again;
Who therewith angry, when it next came there,
Took it in snuff; and still he smiled and talk'd,
And as the soldiers bore dead bodies by,
He call'd them untaught knaves, unmannerly,
To bring a slovenly unhandsome corse
Betwixt the wind and his nobility.
With many holiday and lady terms
He question'd me; amongst the rest, demanded
My prisoners in your majesty's behalf.
I then, all smarting with my wounds being cold,
To be so pester'd with a popinjay,
Out of my grief and my impatience,
Answer'd neglectingly I know not what,
He should, or he should not; for he made me mad
To see him shine so brisk, and smell so sweet,
And talk so like a waiting-gentlewoman
Of guns and drums and wounds,—God save the mark!—
And telling me the sovereign'st thing on earth
Was parmaceti for an inward bruise;
And that it was great pity, so it was,
This villanous salt-petre should be digg'd
Out of the bowels of the harmless earth,
Which many a good tall fellow had destroy'd
So cowardly; and but for these vile guns,
He would himself have been a soldier.

Lord Wavell, another literary man who has seen some military service, selects this passage [1] as depicting the grudge of the regimental officer against the staff officer—'a feeling', he truly says, 'as old as the history of fighting'. The Field Marshal is of course perfectly right in saying that these lines express that sentiment, but the last two of them make it plain that the particular popinjay in question was not a staff officer but a civilian.

Shakespeare's intimate acquaintance with the soldiers of his epoch has received a generous tribute from John Fortescue, the historian of the British Army. 'Shakespeare,' he writes, 'is as truly the painter of the English Army in his own day as was Marryat of the Navy in later years. Falstaff the fraudulent captain, Pistol the swaggering ensign, Bardolph the rascally corporal, Nym the impostor who affects military brevity, Parolles, "the damnable both sides rogue," nay even Fluellen, a brave and honest man but a pedant, soaked in classical affectations and seeking his model for everything in Pompey's camp—all these had their counterparts in every shire of England. . . . Not in these poor pages, but in Shakespeare must the military student read the history of the Elizabethan soldier.' It will be generally agreed that Marryat could never have painted the Navy so accurately if he had not served in it.

Fortescue tells us too how ill Queen Elizabeth treated her soldiers. 'An Act was passed in 1593

---

[1] In his anthology, *Other Men's Flowers*, pp. 130–31.

throwing the relief of crippled or destitute soldiers on their parishes, the Queen could not see what more they could want. Bloody Mary had shown them compassion, not so would Good Queen Bess; she would not be pestered with the sight of the "miserable creatures".' [1] You will remember in *Pericles*—no, you won't, though, for I doubt if you've read it—but there does occur in that play a scene where the immaculate Marina is urging the brothel-keeper's tout to adopt a more honourable profession, and he replies, 'What would you have me do? go to the wars, would you? where a man may serve seven years for the loss of a leg, and have not money enough in the end to buy him a wooden one?'

And in the sonnets, of all places, a similar complaint is expressed in very different language:

The painful warrior famoused for fight,
After a thousand victories once foil'd,
Is from the book of honour razed quite,
And all the rest forgot for which he toil'd.

All classes of the community have their grievances, but it does seem that it was the soldiers who most frequently found their spokesman in Shakespeare. Every effect, they say, must have a cause. I think the cause of Shakespeare's sympathy with soldiers was the fact that he had been one.

---

[1] Hon. J. W. Fortescue, *History of the British Army*, vol. 1, p. 140. *Ibid.*, p. 157.

You ask me why, having put Shakespeare into the army, I have then promoted him to the rank of sergeant. There is one obvious reason. He was not of high enough birth to obtain a commission easily, nor did he stay in the army long enough to earn one. Yet a man of his intelligence was not likely to remain for long a private soldier.

Apart, however, from these good reasons, his military attitude has always seemed to me to be that of a non-commissioned officer, even when he is dealing with commanders-in-chief. One of Othello's first remarks is typical. Anxious to prevent a brawl in the streets of Venice, he exclaims, 'Keep up your bright swords, for the dew will rust them'. Shakespeare did not know much about Venice, where dew is one of the least of inconveniences, but he did know about the care of side-arms, as every well-trained non-commissioned officer must. It is the rebuke that would naturally spring to the lips of one accustomed to correcting such carelessness in private soldiers.

Equally does the last reminiscence of Othello's life recall the N.C.O. rather than the general officer. Having told the messengers what they shall report on his behalf to the senate he adds:

> And say besides, that in Aleppo once,
> Where a malignant and a turban'd Turk
> Beat a Venetian and traduced the state,
> I took by the throat the circumcised dog
> And smote him, thus—

and with these words he gives himself the death-blow.

Such conduct as he here describes would have been highly creditable in a loyal and patriotic N.C.O. who found himself involved in a rowdy scene at a foreign port, but we can hardly imagine circumstances which would justify such behaviour on the part of a highly placed responsible officer. And in the agony of his jealousy when he cries out:

> I had been happy, if the general camp,
> Pioneers and all, had tasted her sweet body,
> So I had nothing known,

it is entirely in accordance with the character of a hard-fighting N.C.O. to think of the pioneers as belonging to a lower order than his fellow soldiers, whereas such nice distinctions in baseness would escape an officer.

What position Enobarbus holds in the army we are never told, but it is certainly a very high one. He is always with Antony and would appear to be either his second-in-command or his chief-of-staff. Pompey says to him, 'I have seen thee fight, when I have envied thy behaviour', and the soldiers who discover his dead body say 'he is of note'. Yet his language throughout and his conduct are those of an N.C.O. rather than a general. The famous speech in which he describes the arrival of Cleopatra by barge is hardly in keeping with his usual utterings, which are coarse, to the point, and often in prose. Menas appears to fill the same role in the entourage of Pompey as Enobarbus does in that of Antony. They should, in fact, both be officers of the highest rank, but when they meet for the first time and make friends, their conversation might be that of two old quartermasters, comparing notes as to who has done best in the profitable profession of war.

Menas. You and I have known, sir.
Enobarbus. At sea, I think.
Menas. We have, sir.
Enobarbus. You have done well by water.
Menas. And you by land.
Enobarbus. I will praise any man that will praise me; though it cannot be denied what I have done by land.
Menas. Nor what I have done by water.
Enobarbus. Yes, something you can deny for your own safety: you have been a great thief by sea.
Menas. And you by land.
Enobarbus. There I deny my land service. But give me your hand, Menas: if our eyes had authority, here they might take two thieves kissing.

After further conversation in the same strain, which is hardly what one would expect at the first meeting between a general and an admiral, and a very frank discussion of their masters' affairs, they go off to have a drink together.

The habit of helping themselves generously to enemy property has been a weakness of English soldiers at all periods. They are probably the least cruel of fighting men, but it cannot be pretended that they are the most honest. Shakespeare confirms what so many have witnessed. The soldier who frightened the French away by shouting 'A Talbot' immediately appropriates the clothes they have left behind, saying:

> I'll be so bold to take what they have left.
> The cry of Talbot serves me for a sword;
> For I have loaden me with many spoils,
> Using no other weapon but his name.

For Shakespeare all soldiers are English [1] soldiers, just as all clowns are Warwickshire clowns, and we are not surprised to find the soldiers of Coriolanus behaving in the same way as those of the Lancastrian kings. In the streets of Corioli while the battle is still in progress we are presented with three Roman soldiers:

First Roman. This will I carry to Rome.
Second Roman. And I this.
Third Roman. A murrain on't! I took this for silver.

Unfortunately for them they are caught in the act

---

[1] Except that boring sapper Fluellen, and his Scotch and Irish companions.

by their general, who has no sympathy with such human weakness:

> See here these movers that do prize their hours
> At a crack'd drachma! Cushions, leaden spoons,
> Irons of a doit, doublets that hangmen would
> Bury with those that wore them, these base slaves,
> Ere yet the fight be done, pack up: down with them!

There are no stage directions after these last words, so we can hope that these poor soldiers escaped the cruel fate of Bardolph and Nym, the former boon companions of Henry V, who were hanged, with his approval, for this same offence of looting. They were indeed 'sworn brothers in filching' and 'would steal any thing, and call it purchase'. In this, his last campaign, 'Bardolph stole a lute-case, bore it twelve leagues, and sold it'. He was doubtless a thief and a coward, but after Falstaff's death he said, 'Would I were with him, wheresome'er he is, either in heaven or in hell'. For that speech alone much should have been forgiven him.

Shakespeare, the dramatist, puts cold, harsh words into the mouths of Coriolanus and Henry V, rightly condemning the offence of looting, but Shakespeare the ex-sergeant cannot help condoning it when committed by such characters as Falstaff or Enobarbus.

There is a further curious item of evidence which points to the limitation of Shakespeare's military experience and confirms the view that it did not extend to the commissioned ranks. The word colonel, or coronel, was beginning officially but not familiarly to be used at the end of the six-teenth century. Fortescue [1] tells us that it was in full use before 1588 and applied to the chief of a regiment, as did the term sergeant-major to the second-in-command. Neither word occurs in the works of Shakespeare, although the words captain, lieutenant, ancient, sergeant and corporal are frequent.

You may think that such an omission on Shake-peare's part argues ignorance of military matters hardly compatible with having served in the army. My slight experience of army life leads me to the opposite conclusion. For the private soldier and the non-commissioned officer the company is a little world in itself, over which the captain [2] rules, and beyond which all is dark and vague. Some-where, far away and high above, there is a general —but he is so distant, like a king, that when Shake-speare comes to deal with him, he relies upon his poetic imagination rather than upon his personal experience. Othello is a general, but, as we have seen, his soldierly qualities are those of a sergeant. Macbeth and Richard III are generals, and fierce fighters, but we never think of them as soldiers.

I remember that, towards the close of that war to which I have already alluded, a benevolent gov-ernment had the bright idea that the education of

---

[1] Fortescue's article on The Army in *Shakespeare's England*, vol. 1, p. 117.

[2] I am told that companies are now—more often than not—commanded by majors—but it was not so in my time, nor in Shakespeare's.

the troops might have been neglected during the four years they had been sitting in the trenches. Instructions therefore filtered down to young officers, employed in maintaining the morale of troops between periods of duty in the line, by inflicting upon them practice in squad-drill, to stand them easy for short intervals, and talk to them about the war and the objects of it, and to find out, by questioning, the extent of their information and the state of their minds. I was, at the time, surprised by the result of my first examination. There were then five British Armies holding the long front line which extended from the English Channel on our left to our French allies on our right. Not one man in my platoon knew to which of those five armies we belonged; not one knew the difference between an army, a corps, and a division; and only one knew the name of the commanding officer of the battalion in which we were serving, and he incorrectly stated it as 'Count Lascelles'.[1] After that experience I am quite willing to believe that young Sergeant Shakespeare, whose teeming brain was occupied with other matters than the military hierarchy, may have ignored the correct style of senior officers with whom he never came into contact.

---

[1] It was, in fact, Viscount Lascelles, subsequently 6th Earl of Harewood.

In all professions there must be competition, and wherever there is competition there must be jealousy. This passion, which corrodes the minds of men, is certainly as prevalent in the military profession as in any other. It is a pity that it should be so, but so it is. The reason may be that it is a profession in which opportunity of proving talent comes so seldom, that those who believe that they possess it may never receive the wholesome correction afforded by experience. Politicians and lawyers are making speeches all the time, and it is soon shown who can make the better one. The same is true of writers, musicians, painters and actors. But those who are employed in the fighting services can only show their true quality in war-time, and wars, though all too frequent, are not perpetual. Even in war the element of luck is ever-present. One man may get a dozen chances and another get none. When a brave soldier, having done his duty, finds himself, at the end of a campaign, passed over in favour of another, who has seen less fighting, but has been more fortunate, and whom he deems his inferior in every way, the bitterness that creeps into his heart is very terrible, and it may fester there until it warps his whole being. Shakespeare, if he served in the army, may have met with a man who suffered from this evil obsession. It is certain that he made of such a man the villain of his most moving tragedy.

Some of the greatest of Shakespearean critics have been puzzled to find the motive for Iago's villainy. In order to explain it Coleridge was driven to invent the phrase 'motiveless malignancy'. Hazlitt found that Iago was 'the dupe and victim of his ruling passion—an insatiable craving after action of the most difficult and dangerous kind'. A. C. Bradley wrote,[1] 'Why did he act as we see him acting in the play? What is the answer to that appeal of Othello's

> Will you, I pray, demand that demi-devil
> Why he hath thus ensnared my soul and body?

This question Why? is *the* question about Iago, just as the question Why did Hamlet delay? is *the* question about Hamlet.' Bradley's conclusion is that Iago could not have answered it himself. And yet the answer is given in what seems to me perfectly intelligible language in the very first words of the play.

Some of our modern writers leave us even at the end of the story in considerable doubt as to what has happened and why. Such was not Shakespeare's way. In all his greatest works he contrives to make the point of the play perfectly plain to the audience from the outset. In *Julius Caesar* we are presented at once with the opposition that is being aroused

---

[1] *Shakespearean Tragedy*, p. 222.

by Caesar's ambition. In *King Lear* we are informed in the first remarks exchanged of the old king's foolish decision to partition his kingdom, and almost simultaneously we are introduced to the sub-plot in the persons of Gloucester and Edmund. *Hamlet* opens with the ghost, and *Macbeth* with the witches. Similarly the first words of *Othello* convey to the audience Iago's hatred of his master and the cause of it—Cassio has been promoted over his head—Cassio,

> That never set a squadron in the field,
> Nor the division of a battle knows
> More than a spinster . . .
>   mere prattle without practice
> Is all his soldiership.

He goes on to complain that

> Preferment goes by letter and affection,
> And not by old gradation, where each second
> Stood heir to the first.

Nobody has ever sat in an army mess for long without hearing this complaint repeated.

Amongst other terms of contempt which Iago applies to Michael Cassio is that he is

> Forsooth, a great arithmetician.

You will understand how those words leapt to my memory when I came upon the following passage in the *History of the British Army*:—'On Leicester's resignation of the chief command [in the Low Countries, in 1586] there was appointed to succeed him a man whose name must ever be venerated in the British Army, Prince Maurice of Nassau, second son of William the Silent. . . . His own natural bent lay chiefly towards mathematics which he cultivated as a means to the mastery of military engineering, and eventually reduced to practice by so sedulous a use of the spade in all military operations as to provoke many a sneer from soldiers of a more primitive type.' [1]

Here surely is something more than a coincidence. Here is a piece of circumstantial evidence that should carry weight with any jury. Shakespeare's patron, Leicester, is recalled from his command, which is taken over by a young prince, notoriously addicted to mathematics. He is sneered at by the troops, and Shakespeare, years afterwards, looking for a term of abuse to put into the mouth of Iago, sneering at a senior officer, lights upon the word 'arithmetician'.[2] Can we not hear in the word itself an echo of what was being muttered round the camp fires that spring in Holland, after the dashing English earl had gone and the cautious Dutch prince had replaced him? Nothing in the play supports the taunt. There is nothing of the arithmetician about Cassio. Shakespeare could have given us a serious-minded, studious staff-officer if he had wished. But instead he gave us the debonair, delightful Cassio, who even in his cups and

---

[1] Fortescue, *History of the British Army*, vol. I, p. 152.
[2] Almost equally striking is the last dying taunt of Mercutio concerning Tybalt, his slayer—'a braggart, a rogue, a villain that fights by the book of arithmetic'.

in his courting commands our affection, and of whom Iago is compelled to say:

> He hath a daily beauty in his life
> That makes me ugly.

Why was Othello blind to that beauty and that ugliness? Why could he not see that Cassio was a gentleman, which Iago never even pretended to be? The reason is obvious—at least it is obvious to those who, like Shakespeare, have served in the army. Officers who have risen from the ranks have often proved the best of leaders and the wisest of generals. But they have one weakness. Outside the war council and off the parade-ground they are never quite sure of themselves. Had Othello been able to say—as in his position he should have said at once—'Look here, Iago, you are a good soldier and an honest fellow, but if you say one more word about her ladyship, I shall have you transferred immediately to another command'—had he said that, there would have been no tragedy, but he could not say it because, having served in the ranks himself, it did not seem to him abominable that the very name of Desdemona should ever be sullied by Iago's lips.

Iago is one of Shakespeare's greatest creations, and it is the fate of creators that they sometimes lose control of their own creatures. It may have happened here. Shakespeare may have intended to create merely a cruel, villainous soldier nursing a bitter grudge, and he found he had whistled up a fiend from hell. Fearing lest the motive should

66

prove inadequate for the crime, he tried, too late, to add another, suggesting as an afterthought that Iago suspected Othello's relations with Emilia, Iago's wife. This far graver cause for hatred is not mentioned until the third scene and is soon forgotten. Iago himself says casually, 'I know not if't be true'; but, in point of fact, he knew very well, as you and I know, that it wasn't. Othello was not that sort of man. So military jealousy remains the sole motive of the villainy, and Shakespeare was satisfied, from his experience, that military jealousy, working on a mind like Iago's, could produce such terrible results.

Has it ever occurred to you that the quarrel scene between Brutus and Cassius in the fourth act of *Julius Caesar* is a very curious interpolation? The play is approaching its climax, which is reached in the next scene on the plains of Philippi. Brutus and Cassius, brothers-in-law, have been the best of friends throughout, and become so again before the scene is ended. Yet there is here introduced a violent quarrel, which has no bearing whatever on the plot and which could not possibly be missed if it were omitted. It never is omitted when the play is acted, because it is as fine a piece of dramatic writing as the author ever produced, and holds the audience spellbound.

And what is it all about? It is a typical soldier's tiff, due to the resentment of Brutus at the attempt of Cassius to 'come the old soldier' over him. When it is all over and they are friends again, Brutus tries to excuse his ill humour on the ground that he had just had news of his wife's death. A worse excuse was never made. Shakespeare, with all his knowledge of the human heart, knew as well as we do that when a man is suffering from profound sorrow he is not likely to be in an irritable or quarrelsome mood. Small matters which might prove a source of friction at other times lose all significance. Earlier in the scene, when Brutus has lost control of himself, he blurts out the real cause of his anger:

> You say you are a better soldier:
> Let it appear so; make your vaunting true,
> And it shall please me well: for mine own part,
> I shall be glad to learn of noble men.

Poor Cassius, who is now quite overwhelmed by the storm he has provoked, understands at last what it is that has so infuriated Brutus, and hastens to excuse himself:

> You wrong me every way; you wrong me, Brutus,

he exclaims,

> I said an elder soldier, not a better:
> Did I say, better?

To which Brutus makes the reply, characteristic of a man whose ill-temper has driven away his reason:

> If you did, I care not.

What Cassius had actually said was:

> I am a soldier, I,
> Older in practice, abler than yourself
> To make conditions.

And at the beginning of the scene, before he had understood how angry Brutus was, he had taken the line of the older and more experienced man explaining matters to one who is in need of instruction. It is an attitude particularly resented by military men, and if Shakespeare had not himself been a military man at one period he could hardly have so accurately described a soldier's quarrel.

It was perhaps due to the quarrel, and to the anxiety with which it left Cassius not to provoke again his irascible brother-in-law, that in the council of war which follows immediately he allows Brutus to have his way. Brutus is one of those admirable, high-minded people who happen to be always wrong. He was wrong when he persuaded the conspirators to spare Antony; he was still more wrong when, against the advice of Cassius, he gave Antony permission to speak in the forum, and now he makes his final and fatal error, in deciding, once more in opposition to Cassius, to march on to Philippi, instead of holding their ground and waiting for the enemy to attack. So Cassius proved, what he claimed to be, the older and the abler soldier of the two.

Do you think that Shakespeare envied the officers who were put over him, and resented the inferiority of his position? I doubt it. Some such feeling may be detected in the lines that occur in *Measure for Measure*:

> That in the captain's but a choleric word,
> Which in the soldier is flat blasphemy.

But it is Isabella speaking and pleading with Angelo for her brother's life, and she has just expressed the same sentiment in other words:

> Great men may jest with saints; 'tis wit in them,
> But in the less foul profanation.

Parolles also has something rude to say about captains:

> Captain I'll be no more;
> But I will eat and drink, and sleep as soft
> As captain shall.

Parolles, however, is a contemptible rogue, as well as a tedious one, and he is the last man through whose mouth Shakespeare would have expressed any of his own feelings. Rather would he have applauded Doll Tearsheet when she trounces Pistol for assuming a rank to which he has no right:

Captain! thou abominable damned cheater, art thou not ashamed to be called captain? An captains were of my mind, they would truncheon you out, for taking their names upon you before you have earned them. You a captain! you slave, for what?

There was nothing of the revolutionary in Shakespeare. Jack Cade was his portrait of a rebel. Somewhere he had come to understand the importance of discipline and the folly of seeking for equality. It is my contention that the army is the best school where such lessons may be learnt.

> The heavens themselves, the planets and this centre,
> Observe degree, priority and place . . . .
>   O, when degree is shaked,
> Which is the ladder to all high designs,
> The enterprise is sick! How could communities,
> Degrees in schools and brotherhoods in cities,
> Peaceful commerce from dividable shores,
> The primogenitive and due of birth,
> Prerogative of age, crowns, sceptres, laurels,
> But by degree, stand in authentic place?
> Take but degree away, untune that string,
> And, hark, what discord follows!

These are the words used by the wise Ulysses while the Greeks are debating outside the walls of Troy how they can capture the city. He goes on to explain how this lack of respect for rank is working havoc in the army:

>   The general's disdain'd
> By him one step below; he by the next;
> That next by him beneath: so every step,
> Exampled by the first pace that is sick
> Of his superior, grows to an envious fever
> Of pale and bloodless emulation.

72

It is interesting to note how Shakespeare avoids giving a name to any rank beneath that of general, which again bears witness to his lack of interest in the higher branches of the profession. But he has understood, as he always did, the heart of the matter, and he applies the lesson that he learnt in the army to the conduct of life in general. He had a soldier-like admiration for leadership. He had learnt the value of it. Already in *Venus and Adonis* we find him writing:

> Like soldiers, when their captain once doth yield,
> They basely fly, and dare not stay the field.

The lesson he had learnt in youth was not forgotten, as two passages in the later plays will show. When the exiled Kent returns, in disguise, to re-enter the service of Lear, he says:

> You have that in your countenance which I would
>   fain call master.
> What's that? [asks the King.]
> Authority.

A similar sentiment is expressed by Aufidius when he finds Coriolanus in his kitchen, a refugee in rags:

> Say, what's thy name?
> Thou hast a grim appearance, and thy face
> Bears a command in't.

The tragedy of Lear was that out of laziness and love of pleasure he laid aside the authority that was inherent in him. The tragedy of Coriolanus was that he sought to rule those whom he despised and hated. A guiltier man than Lear, his punishment was less terrible, and we feel that, unlike Lear, he has learnt nothing at the end of it. He would never have prayed in the midst of storm and darkness for the poor naked wretches, homeless on such a night, nor admit that he had thought too little of them in happier times. It is the duty of some men to command, but their command, whether in war or peace, must be exercised for the benefit of their subordinates.

> O, it is excellent
> To have a giant's strength; but it is tyrannous
> To use it like a giant.

This is the lesson that the army teaches, when every officer is trained to see to the comfort of his men before his own.

Most creative writers make use of their personal experience both in selection of background and portrayal of character. Jane Austen seldom leaves her village, except to call at the great house. Balzac is continually returning to the theme of the young man from the provinces, who comes to make his fortune in Paris. Unhappy children have more than their fair share of the works of Dickens. The effect produced by Europe on the minds of Americans is a favourite subject with Henry James. Examples might be multiplied to show that autobiography forces its way into the works of all imaginative writers.

We have no reason to suppose that Shakespeare formed an exception to this rule. Reading through the list of *dramatis personae* of those thirty-seven plays, we cannot but be astonished at the number of soldiers' names on that immortal roster. Admitting that in the historical plays, classical as well as modern, soldiers impose their presence by the subject of the story, we may yet question why it was necessary to introduce them and the language of their trade, so frequently into plays and poems that had no relish of the military in them. Why should the reverend Friar Lawrence in his cell rebuke Romeo with the words:

Thy wit . . .
Like powder in a skilless soldier's flask
Is set a-fire by thine own ignorance,
And thou dismember'd with thine own defence?

Why should the insufferable Parolles be dragged
into *All's Well That Ends Well*? He plays no part
in the plot, and when the play is nearly over (Act
III, scene 5), we are all taken off to a battlefield, in
order, apparently, to expose the cowardice of
Parolles, about which the audience has never been
in doubt. The stage direction is:

Drum and Colours. Enter Bertram, Parolles, and the
whole army.

The end of *Cymbeline*—you may not agree with
me, and you may remind me that it was the favourite play of both Swinburne and Tennyson—is
spoilt by the introduction of a most unnecessary
and unhistorical war—nothing less, in fact, than the
defeat of the Roman invasion by the ancient Britons.
The fate of the day being turned, as in *The Drums
of the Fore and Aft*, by two boy heroes who, more
fortunate than Kipling's lads, survive the action.

Even in his first poems he cannot throw off this
military obsession. The proudest boast that Venus
makes, in *Venus and Adonis*, is her victory over the
God of War:

Over my altars hath he hung his lance,
His batter'd shield, his uncontrolled crest,
And for my sake hath learn'd to sport and dance,
To toy, to wanton, dally, smile and jest;
  Scorning his churlish drum and ensign red,
  Making my arms his field, his tent my bed.

76

Yet more striking is the obtrusion of the military motif into *The Rape of Lucrece*. The very climax of the story is approaching. The villainous seducer is bending over the sleeping and uncovered form of his victim. He dares for the first time to touch her when suddenly Shakespeare's mind reverts to the sieges of small, fortified towns in the Low Countries—and he embarks on an elaborate military metaphor:

[His veins] like straggling slaves for pillage [1] fighting,
Obdurate vassals fell exploits effecting,
In bloody death and ravishment delighting,
Nor children's tears nor mothers' groans respecting,
Swell in their pride, the onset still expecting:
   Anon his beating heart, alarum striking,
   Gives the hot charge, and bids them do their liking.

His drumming heart cheers up his burning eye,
His eye commends the leading to his hand;
His hand, as proud of such a dignity,
Smoking with pride, march'd on to make his stand
On her bare breast, the heart of all her land;
   Whose ranks of blue veins, as his hand did scale,
   Left their proud turrets destitute and pale.

We cannot fail to be reminded here of a far more sublime moment in the works of Shakespeare, when Romeo looks upon the supposedly dead body of Juliet, and, employing once more the military metaphor, attains the cloudy summit of poetry:

Thou art not conquer'd; beauty's ensign yet
Is crimson in thy lips and in thy cheeks,
And death's pale flag is not advanced there.

---

[1] The loot motif again.

Later in *The Rape of Lucrece* he sends the unhappy heroine to gaze on a celebrated painting of the siege of Troy which is described in ten stanzas. Portraits are drawn of all ranks, including:

> the labouring pioneer
> Begrimed with sweat and smeared all with dust;

and a contrast is drawn between the 'grace and majesty' of the 'great commanders' on the one hand, and on the other the

> Pale cowards, marching on with trembling paces;
> Which heartless [1] peasants did so well resemble
> That one would swear he saw them quake and tremble.

Shakespeare had seen himself those unhappy peasants quaking and trembling, forced to fight against their will, and he had not forgotten them.

---

[1] Heartless means, of course, without courage.

In these early poems and plays the poet is
principally interested in the plot. Psychology was
a word unknown to him—as it remained unknown
to Dr. Johnson—and he was not concerned, as
modern writers are, with the intricate motives at
the root of human behaviour. Critics who seek to
apply the subtlety of Freud to the simplicity of
Shakespeare are wasting their time; the real reason
for the behaviour of his characters being the demands of the story.

But the greatest artists are greater than they
know; the spirit carries them beyond their ken,
and they find they are moving about in worlds
unrealised, even by themselves. So under the
moulding fingers of the young Shakespeare the old
clay that had served time and again to turn out the
familiar puppets of the playhouse gradually, mirac-
ulously, produced living men and women. Here
we are concerned only with one type which as a
type emerges early, and which soon ceases to be a
type and multiplies into a number of individuals,
who resemble one another as human beings often
do, but who are never identical—as human beings
never are. The type I mean is that of the frank,
outspoken soldier, who enjoys life and is full of
courage and common-sense. You heard him speak

first through the mouth of Warwick in the Temple Garden, but as the play continued Warwick faded away into one of the colourless lords of the historical plays, who resemble one another so closely that it seems to matter little to which of them any speech is given.

Between the writing of the last part of *Henry VI* and the first part of *Henry IV* there is a great gulf. Scholars argue as to the works that filled it. I will not weary you with the results of their researches. Nobody can be sure of the truth. Suffice it to say that during those years Shakespeare from a tyro became a master. It is probable that *King John* belongs to that period, and in this play we meet again the type that we are seeking. The Poet Laureate [1] finds the character of the Bastard Faulconbridge 'common', and deplores the fact that he preferred to be the natural son of Richard Coeur-de-Lion rather than the legitimate son of a nobody. I cannot be sure that I understand the sense in which the dangerous word 'common' is here employed, or how the author of *The Widow in the Bye-Street* can apply it to one of Shakespeare's noblest creations. But the opinion of poets must be treated with respect, and Mr. Masefield has much to say about the Bastard that is worth hearing. He maintains that, with two exceptions, 'the Bastard is the most English figure in the plays. He is the Englishman neither at his best nor at his worst, but

[1] John Masefield, *William Shakespeare* (Home University Library).

at his commonest'—(whatever that means)—'The Englishman was never so seen before, nor since. An entirely honest, robust, hearty person, contemptuous of the weak, glad to be a king's bastard, making friends with women (his own mother one of them) with a trusty, good-humoured frankness, fond of fighting, extremely able when told what to do, fond of plain measures—the plainer the better, an honest servant, easily impressed by intellect when found in high place on his own side, but utterly incapable of perceiving intellect in a foreigner, fond of those sorts of humour which generally lead to blows, extremely just, very kind when not fighting, fond of the words "fair play", and nobly and exquisitely moved to deep, true poetical feeling by a cruel act done to something helpless and little.'

Masefield is thinking here of the Bastard's behaviour when the corpse of Prince Arthur is discovered. There are certain lords present, and Hubert, who with just cause is deeply suspected of the murder, arrives. They are for putting him to death at once, but the Bastard, though feeling as deep indignation as any, restrains them from acting without proof. He is left alone with the suspected murderer to whom he says:

> Beyond the infinite and boundless reach
> Of mercy, if thou didst this deed of death,
> Art thou damn'd, Hubert.

In reply to Hubert's protestations of innocence the Bastard tells him to pick up the little boy's body, knowing that such a man as Hubert could not bear to do so if he had been responsible for his death. When he gladly obeys the Bastard acquits him of the crime, exclaiming:

> I am amazed, methinks, and lose my way
> Among the thorns and dangers of this world.
> How easy dost thou take all England up!

Masefield finds these lines 'commonplace', which proves that this word and the word 'common' mean something to him that they do not mean to me. Apart from them his sketch of the Bastard's character is useful, save that he omits the essential point that the man is a soldier. When he first presents himself to the King and the Queen-Mother, John finds him 'a good blunt fellow', but Queen Elinor, who is his grandmother, sees what he is born to be and says:

> I like thee well: wilt thou forsake thy fortune,
> Bequeath thy land to him [1] and follow me?
> I am a soldier and now bound to France.

to which he answers:

> Madam, I'll follow you unto the death.

So he goes to the wars and becomes the hero of the play and the mouthpiece of England.

Hazlitt described the Bastard as 'a comic character', which seems to me almost as strange as to call him 'common'. Supposedly he meant that the Bastard belonged to high comedy rather than to tragedy. He saw, however, the point which Mase-

---

[1] His half-brother, who is legitimate.

field missed, 'The difference between Falconbridge and the other [comic characters in Shakespeare] is that he is a soldier, and brings his wit to bear upon action, is courageous with his sword as well as tongue, and stimulates his gallantry by his jokes, his enemies feeling the sharpness of his blows and the sting of his sarcasms at the same time'.[1]

---

[1] *Characters of Shakespear's Plays*, 1817, p. 252.

If Faulconbridge is a soldier, first and last, the same is not true of Prince Hal, afterwards Henry V. His is a more complicated and less admirable character. He serves rather as an example of the kind of youth who needs military discipline to make a man of him. He has courage and love of adventure in abundance. These are the qualities which, until they are harnessed, drive him into wild courses. But even while he is pursuing them he is dreaming of how he will redeem all his follies on the battlefield

> in the closing of some glorious day.

The battle of Shrewsbury gives him his chance, of which he takes full advantage, overcoming in single combat the gallant Harry Percy, who is the more military minded of the two, and whom his wife reproaches for talking in his sleep:

> Of sallies and retires, of trenches, tents,
> Of palisadoes, frontiers, parapets,
> Of basilisks, of cannon, culverin,
> Of prisoners' ransom, and of soldiers slain.

A lesser writer would have reformed the Prince after his heroic exploits. Shakespeare knew better. Bad habits are not so easily laid aside. The gay company return straight from the battlefield to the tavern in Eastcheap where the Prince is with them, and the fun is faster than ever. A greater shock, namely his father's death and his succession, was required to

> whip the offending Adam out of him.

Modern sentiment is pained by his desertion of his old friends. I am not sure that Shakespeare would have shared our feelings. Dickens would have settled Falstaff down with a pension in a country cottage with honeysuckle growing round the door, and a hospitable inn hard-by where the old gentleman, grown quite respectable, would have recounted tales of the riotous past to the wondering yokels, and where perhaps the King would have paid him an occasional visit. But Shakespeare did not live in a sentimental age. For him Falstaff remained a wicked man, who deserved to be punished, and when Queen Elizabeth asked for a play about Falstaff in love, Shakespeare, who knew that Falstaff could never be in love, wrote a farce about a fat clown and called him Falstaff, but he was no relation to the friend of Prince Hal who fought at Shrewsbury.

I hear your reproach. I am wandering from my subject. Falstaff led me astray. He was ever a tempter and he is mighty yet.

When Henry V put on his crown he got into uniform and never took it off again. It is true that he still played pranks, as on the eve of Agincourt, but they are tedious ones, typical of the bad young man who has 'made good'. There is something almost affected about this King's desire to be taken for a soldier and nothing else. When he is left alone with the French King's daughter, whom everybody knows he intends to marry for political reasons, he begins his courtship by:

> Will you vouchsafe to teach a soldier terms
> Such as will enter at a lady's ear
> And plead his love-suit to her gentle heart?

and he continues in the same strain:

I speak to thee plain soldier . . . If thou would have such a one, take me; and take me, take a soldier.

He goes on to say that he hopes she will prove a good soldier-breeder. She proved, as we know, a very poor one. But the interesting point is that this great king, who had just conquered France, made it his proudest boast that he was a plain soldier. Whether we like him or not, I think that Shakespeare liked him, and wrote of him in good faith, without satire, and that, if he was proud to be a soldier, Shakespeare shared his pride.

There remains one more of Shakespeare's soldiers who demands our attention, but before dealing with him I had better tell you frankly that of all Shakespeare's plays *Coriolanus* is the one which pleases me least. I may be wrong; you will say I must be, when you learn that so high an authority as Mr. T. S. Eliot [1] takes the opposite view. He considers it to be—together with *Antony and Cleopatra*—'Shakespeare's most assured artistic success'. He therefore compares it with *Hamlet*, very much to the latter's disadvantage, for *Hamlet* is, in his opinion, 'most certainly an artistic failure'.

But then he accepts with regard to *Hamlet* the views of J. M. Robertson, a gentleman who, by the way, believed that the main 'draftsman' of *Romeo and Juliet* was George Peele,[2] who received, of course, assistance in the task from that ubiquitous committee Greene, Marlowe and Kyd. Robertson succeeded in convincing Mr. Eliot that Shakespeare's *Hamlet* was founded·upon an earlier, lost, play by Thomas Kyd, of whom no

---

[1] *Selected Essays*, p. 141.
[2] Chambers, vol. 1, p. 345. It must not be supposed that Sir Edmund Chambers supports Robertson's theory. He merely records it.

quite certain works remain, and that such famous passages as the oft-quoted advice given by Polonius to Laertes were lifted from Kyd, having been amended by Chapman on the way. Kyd, it seems, had written a rattling good play about revenge, and then Shakespeare must come along with his Oedipus Complex and spoil it all by superimposing a psychological study—'the essential emotion of the play being the feeling of a son towards a guilty mother'.

It is to be hoped that admirers of Mr. Eliot in the days to come, if they are as ingenious as modern scholars, will be able to reattribute this particular essay to some obscure Freudian practitioner, proving conclusively from internal evidence that it cannot possibly be by the hand of the master.

It is the character of Coriolanus himself which detracts from the interest of the play. The central figure of a great tragedy must have some fascination. We shudder at, but also with, Macbeth. We hold his trembling hand as he wades into blood and share his horror of it. Even Richard III has a hideous glamour for us, as he had for the Lady Anne whose husband he had murdered. But who can care for Coriolanus?

You will know that I do not dislike him because he was a patrician, who despised the mob. Indeed, I find little of the true patrician about him. He was always losing his temper and beating the servants. He was in my opinion the type of officer who, in spite of many good qualities, brings discredit upon the fighting services. Brave, efficient and modest about his real achievements, he sought political power without the tact or patience to acquire it, and was inordinately proud of his caste. Reckless of his own life, he set no store by the lives of others, and therefore failed to win the affection, or even the confidence, of his men. A traitor to his country, he betrayed his new employers, and richly merited his fate.

Although a young officer's heart may beat faster at the thought of war, and although he may be forgiven for dreaming of glory, I never knew an experienced soldier who did not regard war with profound horror.[1] Not so Coriolanus. In the first scene, on learning that the enemy are in arms, he exclaims:

> I am glad on't: then we shall ha' means to vent
> Our musty superfluity.

By which he means that he hopes a great number of his fellow-countrymen will be killed.

I hope I am as far from being a member of the Peace Pledge Union as I am from being a supporter of the plebs, but a man who rejoices at the outbreak of war and who despises the poorer citizens, soldiers and civilians alike, is a man for whom I can feel nothing but disgust and loathing.

His detestable character was no doubt inherited

---

[1] Stephen Walsh, first Labour Secretary of State for War, is said to have reported to his colleagues, after a few weeks at the War Office, that he had discovered to his astonishment that all the generals were pacifists.

from his mother, Volumnia, the most unsympathetic type of colonel's wife ever portrayed in fiction. Do you remember the words she uses when, he being away at the war, she is discussing him with his sweet, gentle wife?

> Methinks I see him stamp thus, and call thus:
> 'Come on, you cowards! you were got in fear,
> Though you were born in Rome.'

Can you imagine worse evidence against an officer than that his own mother should imagine that his most probable attitude at the front should be taunting his men with cowardice? And she was right; for that was what happened. His men refused to follow him—so much for his gift of leadership—and he went on alone to what must have seemed almost certain death or capture—a most improper action on the part of the second-in-command of a large army.

Volumnia would doubtless have approved, for when they hear he is wounded his unhappy wife exclaims:

> O, no, no, no—

but his loving mother says:

> O, he is wounded; I thank the gods for't.

and when his return is announced with shouts and flourishes she rejoices to think that:

> before him he carries noise, and behind him he leaves tears.

We can guess the kind of education Coriolanus received from that which Volumnia is giving to his little son, of whom she says with pride:

He had rather see the swords and hear a drum than look upon his schoolmaster.

and then her friend, Valeria, relates the following charming anecdote about the child:

O' my word, the father's son: I'll swear, 'tis a very pretty boy. O' my troth, I looked upon him o' Wednesday half an hour together; has such a confirmed countenance. I saw him run after a gilded butterfly; and when he caught it, he let it go again; and after it again; and over and over he comes, and up again; catched it again: or whether his fall enraged him, or how 'twas, he did so set his teeth, and tear it; O, I warrant, how he mammocked [1] it!

'One on's father's moods', exclaims the delighted Volumnia.

I fear I should have been out of sympathy with three generations of the Coriolanus family. How different they are from the gay and care-free military figures of the early plays! How different is this vulgar old termagant from the adorable young Lady Percy, who calls her gallant husband 'mad-headed ape' and 'paraquito', and threatens to break his little finger if he won't tell her his secrets! In what a different mood from any ever known to Coriolanus was Henry V when he prayed for his men on the eve of Agincourt—and in what different words did he exhort them! Had some of the bitterness of Timon entered temporarily into the heart of Shakespeare and turned him so much against the human race that he forgot his old affection for soldiers? I prefer not to believe it, and

---

[1] Tore in pieces.

91

I like to remember that even Timon, at his most miserable, living like an animal on the sea-shore, when he discovered gold refused it to everybody, yet 'enriched poor straggling soldiers with great quantity'. Shakespeare had to show all, the bad as well as the good, and his gallery of military portraits would be incomplete without the forbidding countenance of Coriolanus.

I cannot think that, much as you admire Mr.
Eliot's work, you will share his opinion that
Hamlet is most certainly an artistic failure. I
would ask you rather to share mine—and there
are those who agree with me—that *Hamlet* is the
greatest artistic success of the greatest literary
artist that ever lived. May I, then, draw your
attention to a facet of that rare jewel which usually
escapes notice? It has a dim but pervading military
background. It is very little emphasized, but the
general impression conveyed by the play would
be different without it. You know how a certain
ingredient in a dish, garlic or vinegar or whatever
it may be, itself entirely escaping notice, may yet
so affect the flavour of the whole that its absence
would be at once detected by a sensitive palate.

There is a danger arising 'out of his weakness
and his melancholy' that Hamlet might be thought
effeminate, and he is sometimes played so by effeminate actors. (I find it hard to believe that Sarah
Bernhardt was good in the part, although I suppose
we must take Maurice Baring's word for it.)
Shakespeare, lest we should fall into this error,
slips in occasionally a pinch of the military as a
corrective, like an occasional drum-tap in a great
orchestration.

The first scene is full of conversation, about warlike preparations, and in that solemn moment when, his brain still reeling from the interview with his father's ghost, Hamlet enjoins absolute secrecy on his companions, it is upon his sword he makes them swear, and he exacts the oath from them as 'friends, scholars and soldiers'. Later in the play, when he has consented to go to England, and we might well believe that he had abandoned the dread duty laid upon him, it is the sight of an army that recalls him to his task. Prince Fortinbras, the nephew of old Norway, is marching against Poland. Hamlet enquires the cause of the war, and finds it is as trivial as such causes can be. His reaction, however, is not 'What fools these mortals be!' but rather:

> How all occasions do inform against me,
> And spur my dull revenge!

Far from despising the soldiers and their leader, he admires them; and exalts their willingness to risk their lives for so small a cause while he, with so great a one, still hesitates:

> Examples gross as earth exhort me:
> Witness this army, of such mass and charge,
> Led by a delicate and tender-prince.
>
> . . . .
>
> Exposing what is mortal and unsure
> To all that fortune, death and danger dare,
> Even for an egg-shell.
>
> . . . .

94

> to my shame I see
> The imminent death of twenty thousand men,
> That for a fantasy and trick of fame
> Go to their graves like beds.

He speaks of them, not with contempt, but with admiration. The play then hastes to its conclusion and, when the tragedy is over, Fortinbras appears once more and gives his orders:

> Let four captains
> Bear Hamlet, like a soldier, to the stage;
> For he was likely, had he been put on,
> To have proved most royally: and, for his passage,
> The soldiers' music and the rites of war
> Speak loudly for him.
> . . . Go, bid the soldiers shoot.

These are the last words. The last stage direction of a play which begins with a sentry's challenge is 'a peal of ordnance is shot off'. You may not have noticed it before, but will you not now admit that there runs through *Hamlet*, like a faint military accompaniment, 'the rumble of a distant drum'?

So from the beginning until near the end there is to be traced throughout the works of Shakespeare this curious preoccupation with the military. The military metaphor which continually crops up, even in places where its employment seems hardly suitable, would not prove so powerful an argument if it were not supported by the large number of soldiers who are brought upon the stage, and the sympathy and understanding with which they are presented. The number of nautical metaphors is impressive. But in all the plays, full as they are of foreign travel, I cannot remember a single sailor who can be said to make his number. The ship-master, the boatswain and the sailors make but a poor showing in *The Tempest*, and in *Pericles*, full as it is of shipwreck and the sea, no nautical character emerges. In *Twelfth Night* Antonio is described as a sea-captain, but, although he proves a good friend to Sebastian, there is nothing of the old salt about him, not the faintest whiff of a sea breeze. Those who will have none of my theory may contend that Shakespeare's accuracy about soldiers comes from the fact that he must have met many of them. But he must also have met many sailors, and in those days when discovery was still opening up the world before the eyes of the astonished Elizabethans, when America seemed further away than fairyland, when Drake had just put a girdle round about the earth, how far more interesting to a fertile imagination must have seemed a sailor who had visited the still-vex'd Bermoothes than a soldier who had recently returned from Holland! At all periods, the sailor has been a popular and romantic figure, but never so popular and so romantic as in the days of Raleigh and Hawkins, the Spanish Main and the discovery of the new world. Yet we search the pages of Shakespeare in vain for a single one of these characters whom we most closely associate with the days of Elizabeth.

Legal metaphors are also frequent, but I have read that Shakespeare's law is amateurish, and nearly every reference that he makes to the profession is disparaging. Yet the works of Balzac and Dickens are full of lawyers, good and bad: which proves that they provide suitable material for the dramatic writer. Shakespeare, however, was plainly not interested in legal characters, which surely he would have been if he had been a lawyer himself. He appears to have thought that a pretty girl in disguise could beat the best of them and explain the laws of Venice to the Doge himself.

His interest in military matters seems to have diminished as he grew older—'Old men forget', and, although he was never old, it is thought that he had suffered deeply. He had lost perhaps that gusto which he had brought with him from the camp, and which had come to be replaced by a resigned tranquillity. He had travelled far. Between Falstaff and Prospero there lies a whole universe of human experience. *The Tempest* is thought to be his last play. It is the only one in which I cannot discover a single military metaphor or allusion.

Have I convinced you? I have almost convinced myself. Few writers have been writers all their lives, and nothing else. Once Shakespeare started writing, and acting, his time was full, and there was none to spare for any other activity. But there remain those years to be accounted for, of which we have no knowledge, and during which he was certainly acquiring experience. I cannot believe he was a country schoolmaster, teaching instead of learning. If he had been, he would surely, somewhere in the plays, have produced a schoolmaster whom we should have loved. Holofernes in *Love's Labour's Lost* and Sir Hugh Evans in *The Merry Wives of Windsor* are figures of mockery. There occurs in *The Comedy of Errors* for a brief moment that curious character, who is described in the First Folio as 'a schoolmaster, called Pinch'. He has nothing of the pedagogue about him. His few remarks would seem to be those of either a doctor or a clergyman, and he disappears as mysteriously as he came. Even if there were no place for a schoolmaster in the plays, Shakespeare would have found occasion to say something memorable about that honourable and ill-rewarded profession, had he belonged to it. Yet who can say? Mallarmé was a schoolmaster and so, for a while, was Verlaine. What

might Shakespeare not have been? The words
of the old nursery jingle hum in my memory—

Soldier, sailor, ...

He might have been a soldier like Cervantes, or a
sailor like Marryat, a tinker like Bunyan, a rich
man like Byron or a poor man like Burns. He
might have been an apothecary like Keats, or a
beggar-man like Homer, or even, like Villon, a
thief. The only thing he could not possibly have
been was a shifty Lord Chancellor, who betrayed
his benefactor, wrote exquisite little essays and
took bribes. He remains an enchantment and a
mystery, the heart of which we shall not easily
pluck out.

I have finished. This little book has been written to amuse you, and if it has done so, it has
fulfilled its purpose, my dear.

Château de St. Firmin.   July 1949.